The Carbon Butterfly | Yaniv Izaki

Producer & International Distributor
eBookPro Publishing
www.ebook-pro.com

The Carbon Butterfly
Yaniv Izaki

Translation from the Hebrew by Jerry Hyman

Contact: yaniv@izaki.io
ISBN 9798690972103

THE

CARBON
BUTTERFLY

Innovative Entrepreneurship
in Times of Chaos

YANIV IZAKI

CONTENTS

Entrepreneurship as a way to deal with reality

The present moment is all we have; all else is illusion. Power, fame, and riches all provide a measure of satisfaction for a while, but over time their worth diminishes.

In my view, life should be based on friendship, goodwill, love and self-fulfillment. They are my foundation for a full and happy life. However, the most valuable component we all have is time. It is a vanishing resource.

At the age of 12, I found out the hard way that the time allotted to me was not to be taken for granted. Toward the end of elementary school, after two years of terrible physical pain and memories erased by trauma, Prof. Nadir Arber diagnosed that I was suffering from Crohn's, a chronic bowel disease.

"Yaniv, you have to understand that this will affect your life in lots of ways," Professor Arber intoned softly. "You will need regular medication; you won't be able to eat many different types of foods, and you won't be drafted into the army like everyone else."

My parents looked troubled, but I was actually relieved. The doctors had finally found out what my problem was; it could be treated, and I could go on with my life. From then on, time had new value for me, and I was not going to waste it.

The title of this story links the "Butterfly Effect" to the carbon element and combines them, creating something new.

The "Butterfly Effect" is a concept in Chaos Theory. It is intended to illustrate how one tiny action can lead to a global chain of events, such as how the flutter of a butterfly's wings on one side of the earth can lead to the creation of a tornado on the other. Sometimes, one tiny virus can disrupt the entire modern world, destroying some industries and creating new ones in the process.

Carbon is the most common chemical found in nature. In its pure form it appears in two contrasting forms: as graphite, one of nature's softest materials, and diamond, the hardest material found in nature. Using advanced technology, carbon atoms have been produced into fibers, which can be interwoven to create composite materials that are used, for example, to build aircraft that are light, sturdy, and durable. Each single carbon fiber is a fragile substance, but the process it goes through turns it into something solid and long lasting.

The quarantine period we have all experienced has allowed us to discover new things about ourselves. I have found that you need to take action, to cooperate with others to try to change the world, and most especially, while enjoying every moment of the journey.

This story is intended to give you a glimpse into my experience, the exponential process of growth through the founding of a venture, in this unique time. I hope I can inspire you, make you question reality, and not be afraid to take action to realize your goals.

Yaniv Izaki, *entrepreneur*

CHAPTER 1

Denial

"Idan, are you crazy? You know that three months from now everybody in the world will either be healthy, sick, or dead, right?"

How naive I was... and how wrong!

Saturday, March 28, 2020. Late at night. A video call on the Paris-Tel Aviv line.

My cousin Idan, working at the foreign ministry in security for Israeli flights in Paris, had lots of time to let his thoughts wander. The only flights for Israel during this period were Israeli rescue flights, and that night he called me on video.

"Listen Yaniv! I had a dream last night... we are going to save the Israeli economy!"

During that month, in the light of the notorious wave of layoffs and unpaid leave, I spent most of my free time motivating my friends to take advantage of the opportunity to start projects and try something new. The main goal was to not get sucked into Netflix until they went out of their minds. That same week they came up with seven ideas for new projects, but when Idan called me and made that statement, I couldn't help it, and I laughed in his face.

"I'm glad I amuse you. But just focus for a minute and listen: Unlike you guys in high-tech, most people can't work from home on their computers. They were either fired or forced on unpaid leave because of the fear of mass infection. The government announced a lockdown and only essential workers continue to go to work with certain limitations. I think it's possible to bring people back to work if they have already gotten over the virus. Right now there are several thousand diagnosed patients, but as time goes on there will be more people who get the virus and recover, until they come up with a vaccine, and that will take at least a year."

"At the same time, entire industries rely on manual labor, like manufacturing and shipping. More than that, there are industries that today need more workers urgently, like agriculture and logistics. Employers are limited in the number of employees they can bring to the workplace because of the uncertainty and the risk of an outbreak of infection."

"What I propose is that we set up a website that puts people who have recovered from the virus in contact with business owners who need workers. Win-win situation!"

"Okay Idan, that sounds like the beginning of a start-up... But let's say we do this project and we can connect virus-recovered workers with business owners, what's the point? The Ministry of Health will decide what's the right thing to do. What do we know?"

"Maybe we're not health experts, but the economy is collapsing. We have to try to save the economy!" Idan insisted. "Something has got to be done!"

Deep down, I knew he was right.

I got a fever and a sore throat right after Purim week-end in early March 2020. In retrospect, I found out that I had been exposed to Patient number 171, something I learned after the epidemiologic investigation was published a week after I was exposed to 171. I went into quarantine for a week. Although the symptoms went away, I called the MDA, the Public Health services to come and test me for the virus. After all, what were the odds that 48 hours after exposure to someone with the virus that I would suddenly get a fever and a sore throat?

Three days later, a young woman from MDA Health services came to my apartment. She was pretty, as far as I could tell beneath the biohazard protective gear she wore. She told me to turn my head to the side, took a throat swab, then one from the nose, and immediately fled the apartment.

From my balcony I yelled out to her, "When will I get the results?" "Three days, tops," she replied, "and if you are tested positive, then probably before!"

Very reassuring, for sure.

Thursday evening, three days after the sampling, and no answer. I thought to myself they have to give me an answer soon, I'm going out of isolation on Sunday. If I have the virus and they don't give me instructions before my quarantine is over, it will be medical negligence. And if I didn't get answers in a timely manner, what happens to thousands of other people who don't even know if they're a danger to the public?

After a series of frantic phone call inquiries it was discovered that a mistake had been made. They had entered my ID number incorrectly.

"We are happy to inform you that you are not infected with the virus!" said the technician who had finally located my test sampling. This same sampling had bounced between MDA, the Ministry of Health and the HMO.

"I'm happy to hear it!" I lied into the phone, a grim furrow in my brow. At that moment I was shaken, because I had been made aware of a much more problematic reality: There would be many more human errors along the way, which is understandable. The burden on health authorities had reached proportions that no one in my generation could remember.

By this point I had lost confidence in the system. I realized that in order to change reality one had to be a rebel, and to act.

Idan gave me an unmistakable look over the video call.

It was already two in the morning. I took a deep breath and said: "You found your partner and investor. Let's save the economy."

CHAPTER 2

Anger

"Wait, Izaki, that's crazy Fake News! The antibody tests alone are worthless!"

At the same time, rumors began of rapid antibody testing for the virus, which in the meantime have been administered only to government officials. Logically, if there are antibodies then there is immunity to the virus. So why is the government not able to provide antibody testing for the general public?

By this point I had already lost patience. If the state does not do it, I'll try to find a way to get the work done.

I supposed that in order for the venture to be relevant, it would be necessary to import antibody tests. At least a million of them. In a brief analysis of cost versus benefit, I came to the conclusion that it was worth the price. Cost-benefit analysis has always been my way of perceiving reality. That's how it is when you grow up in the shadow of hospitals. I felt I should never miss out on a moment in life. No one guarantees tomorrow you'll be around to enjoy it.

I became a teaching assistant at the university where I had studied, the Interdisciplinary Center in Herzliya. There I met Dr. Shiri Zemah Shamir, who saw reality in the prism of cost-benefit analysis vis-à-vis the world and sustainability. She always tried to coax me into becoming a researcher. The love of knowledge and new discoveries are precious to her.

"Inditzky, I need your brain for the next two weeks for an important project."

Gilad Inditzky had been recognized as an astute intellect from our high school days. He would always analyze reality in ways that were hard for others to grasp. I asked him to go through the US FDA website, and find all antibody tests for the virus that had been approved.

Bingo. He found one.

Fortunately, I had an account on the Chinese social network WeChat, so I was able to correspond with the Global Sales Manager, based in China.

We found out the hard way that trading with the Chinese who produce the only antibody test with US FDA approval is a task for the Mossad to take on.

The last thing I wrote to the sales agency in China was: "At first you said that there was already one exclusive supplier and you were about to sign an agreement with him. Two days later, you said that there were already three different suppliers to Israel, and now you say you can't export the test for the virus because of the Chinese government's own ban?"

We had hit the Wall of China.

Total failure, but that wasn't the worst of it.

"Izaki, listen. Now that I've read the clinical study of the antibody testing, I understand why the Ministry of Health hasn't imported the tests up until now."

Maybe I had lost confidence in the system too soon?

"Antibody testing determines whether the person examined has antibodies in his blood. But it is known that the body begins to produce antibodies in the early stages of the disease, and not just after full recovery. Do you understand what that means?"

"The truth is, I don't, Indi. Explain."

"It means that if the antibody test is positive, there are two possibilities - either you are cured and you are immune from further infection, or you are carrying the disease, with or without any symptoms, and you are contagious!"

Fuck.

"In short, then, Indi, if someone tests negative for the virus and also positive for the antibody test, is he immune?"

He thought for a few moments before responding: "It's just a theory, because we are assuming that someone who has recovered can't get the virus again."

Two days later, it was reported on the news that in South Korea, 91 civilians had fallen ill for a second time, after being declared as having been cured.

Entering chaos.

CHAPTER 3

Bargaining

"Forget those little projects, we have a real opportunity here to make history. Are you with us?"

Titi Aynaw, a social entrepreneur and model, who was also Miss Israel in 2013 and a "Survivor" reality show graduate, phoned me up at night and said excitedly: "I have a startup idea! I want to set up an exclusive matchmaking website during the quarantine! People will finally be able to get to know each other really well and not just because of their looks!"

We had connected at the university during our undergraduate studies, both studying Sustainability. Titi's second major was Governmental studies, while mine was Economics. A Miss Israel who really works to try to change the world and doesn't just talk about it. I couldn't believe it at first.

"Say, could you please help me study for the exam on Environmental Regulation and Globalization?" She asked shyly.

We sat down to study, and for three straight hours she absorbed material from one of the most complicated courses leading to the degree.

She passed her test successfully, and I was impressed...

"Are you serious or is this an April Fool's joke? Just last week, I was added to four 'exclusive' matchmaking sites 'in the shadow of the pandemic.'"

"'No-oh Izaki, this is a good idea! Maybe we can finally find you a girlfriend so you can relax a little, and maybe even get to sleep like a normal human being."

Titi was making fun of my experiments trying to reach maximum focus. I had concentrated on the "Polyphasic

Sleep" method. I figured that the first step in controlling time is simply to produce more of it. During the experiment, I discovered that I performed best for a long period of time if I wake up before the birds, after four and a half hours of sleep at night. Sometimes, on more challenging days, I added another hour and a half siesta to clear my head.

That's how I was able to stay in focus throughout most of the day and night, making more time for myself and controlling it.

My ex-girlfriends never cared for it. They preferred to dream instead.

"Titi, I have another suggestion for you. Are you listening?"

It was less than a week ago that Idan and I had been trying to figure out how to spread the word and who would be the presenter of the project. The penny dropped for me.

"I have a cousin who works in Paris. He came up with

an idea on how to free us from the quarantine. It will take some hard work and there is a major possibility it will fail... but we have to try."

I told her about the opportunity, the challenges, and the fears. I told her everything.

"It's a brilliant idea, Izaki. I want to be a part of it!"

It was already one in the morning. "Hold the line a minute... and switch to a video call."

"Idan, put a shirt on. Titi Aynaw is waiting on the line. She wants to hear more about the idea."

The three of us spoke for an hour about the idea, the vision, and the goals. We came to the realization that we needed to act in order to change the reality ourselves.

Maybe Titi won't find a match for me for now, and even if there is no romance in my life in the meantime, at least I will try to save the world of other lovers.

CHAPTER 4

Depression

"But if there is no reliable checklist anywhere in the world, how can this initiative help?"

Because I was exempt from the draft, I volunteered. During the first part of the process I told the army doctor: "Doctor, I am color blind."

He answered me with indifference, "Well, then you won't be able to be a pilot." In the end, I proved him wrong. Although it took a few years, after 300 hours of flying, I'm happy to say that I'm a pilot.

The first thing a flight instructor teaches is to go through the aircraft checklist before a flight. My instructors always said that "90% of mid-flight failures are prevented by on-the-ground checks." We don't forego the checklist, not even in a flight simulator.

As with aviation, we understood that to make sure there are no serious errors in our identification process of employee immunity, we needed a uniform checklist that met the standards of the World Health Organization, or at least the Israeli Ministry of Health.

Every country in the world has chosen a different way to deal with the health crisis, and with different response timing. Some nations decided to close their borders hermetically, some invested in an extensive battery of tests for the entire population, some left everything open and only isolated those with a weak immune system. Some said it was just the flu, and regretted saying that very quickly. One day the whole story will be told about this pandemic, as today it is told about the nuclear leak at the Chernobyl nuclear power plant.

Our problem is the uncertainty and fear that dominate. Most of the world's leaders are trying to strengthen their political positions, exploiting the crisis to control public opinion, or reinforcing governmental powers using the "emergency" pretext, at the expense of their citizens. Cost-benefit analysis and health risk management by non-scientists politicians are, at the very least, irresponsible. Perhaps the World Health Organization will put things in order?

Unfortunately, due to the uncertainty, the World Health Organization is not prepared to create a checklist until it has absolute certainty on the subject. If ordinary regulators are risk-averse, the World Health Organization probably invented the definition of "risk aversion".

There is a chance that fear itself will kill us all.

Every entrepreneur is familiar with the phrase 'Done is better than Perfect,' but the problem is that in medicine and when dealing with human mortality it probably isn't enough.

We're stuck.

The conclusion is clear: There is a lack of communication and a lack of transparency between global and national health agencies and the populace. We realized that before we even started to issue immunity certificates to people, information needed to be made available. This was paramount.

We needed to set up a scientific reconnaissance team for the venture. An objective, trustworthy team to find the vital information in a sea of fake news and make it accessible to the general public. Suddenly a friend from high school, who could help, came to my mind.

"Yaniv, it's really very flattering, but I'm still just studying for my doctorate, and I'm getting ready for the birth of my second son in about two weeks... I'm not sure I can lead the scientific team of the venture right now," so said (soon to be Dr.) Roni Sverdlov-Arzi.

Roni is a doctoral student in the Technion, researcher in the Nano-Pharmaceutical Materials Lab, graduated B.Sc. in Chemistry and a master's degree in Nano-Material Engineering. As a student, she had worked for 'Teva,' the pharmaceutical company during the firm's golden years before the troubles began.

I would call her a genius. She would deny it.

My mother, Dr. Yael Izaki, founded 'Netta' - The Center for Career Development, a nonprofit organization operating in the private and public sectors with the aim of helping women realize their professional aspirations. One of the problems I learned from her research was that women often would not apply for a position if they did not have every one of the background requirements. Men usually did the opposite, jumping at the chance and learning along the way.

We constantly see that businesses and nations that have a high percentage of women in key roles are more successful than those who do not. It used to be said that this is about giving an equal opportunity. Today it is clearly a strategic advantage.

"Roni, I have no doubt whatsoever that you can do it. Moreover, I'm sure you'll do a great job. It is entirely up to you, just know that we need to start as soon as possible. Time is not on our side. Set your inner entrepreneur free and run this team! It will change the lives of us all."

10 seconds of quiet on the line.

"Are you still there?"

"Yes. I'm here. I can't guarantee I will succeed but I'd love to join you. Let's start tomorrow. I have to put my son to bed."

We had gained a strategic asset for the venture, and more importantly, the world had gained a scientist and brilliant initiator. We need them badly.

CHAPTER 5

Acceptance

"Yaniv, you have made an interesting proposal here. If you succeed in closing a deal with the State of Israel, you will partner with me in the technology."

I spoke with Dr. Roey Tzezana, a brilliant futurist, about world developments in the aftermath of the global crisis. I asked for his opinion on our joint venture for connecting workers and employers in the shadow of the epidemic. He told me of a similar venture underway, and suggested that I speak to the 'Technologist.'

The Technologist had recently set up a risk management startup, to be used for virus detection tests at the required level of certainty to meet international border requirements at airports. "Not only that," said the Technologist during his presentation to Idan and to me: "We plan to embed this idea now to become a digital vaccine certificate for the new world order, to be used as a passport, a permit to enter public buildings, shops and so on..."

We spoke for about an hour about risk mitigation, game theory models, and the conduct of nations. Opening the world. This is what the technology partner's DNA sounds like.

At the end of the presentation, we asked him: "What does it take for this to happen in Israel?"

The Technologist paused, swallowed and answered, "Listen, Israel is problematic. There is a lot of ego and chest thumping between government ministries and it is unclear who is responsible... Even the Mossad thinks it's the Ministry of Health. I am a proud Israeli, but Israel does not excel in orderly management."

Idan and I silently concurred.

He went on: 'We are in contact with various governments, which are not working fast enough, unfortunately. In addition, we would need two million dollars to start a pilot program in any country."

That's a serious amount of capital to raise immediately, especially at a time when venture capitalists have closed the taps on new investment. They need to salvage their own ventures first.

"This technology sounds like something that suits the immunity project in Israel, but you need funding and an initial country to be a customer. I suggest the following deal: We can raise the money, and perhaps more importantly, we can also make a deal with the State of Israel to conduct the pilot. In return, we want a technology partnership. Do we have a deal?"

The Technologist stared intently at us via the computer screen and finally affirmed, "Agreed, let's do it."

We're going for the jackpot.

I felt the adrenaline in my body, just as I had as a 20-year-old soldier, when I brought my project to the unit commander for approval to have it adopted by the rest of the unit's bases.

My first startup.

I served as a volunteer in the Intelligence Corps, part of a small team with big ideas. We had the freedom to try new things. In my position for the first two years of service, I noticed a major problem in the management of organizational knowledge. With no technical experience, armed only with an understanding of the problem and the solution that was needed, I decided to create order out of the tremendous amount of information. Later I found out that this is called Big Data.

I learned from YouTube tutorials on information management systems, and dived deep into the systems that were open to me. A week passed, and some of the soldiers began to take an interest, and asked what I was doing. When I explained to them that I wanted to create order out of chaos, most of them laughed and said I was wasting my time and energy, because the army is the most inefficient entity in the world.

Two of them believed in me and the idea from the first moment - the young soldier Shlomi Rahima, and a brand new officer - second lieutenant Noa Gosher.

Shlomi Rahima was a highly motivated young programmer who was looking for a challenge to further develop his skills. He turned out to be a good choice, because today he's a Google software engineer.

Dr. Noa Gosher, a young medical doctor who is currently working hospital shifts, had been in a similar position to mine before embarking on the officer training school. She knew the problem I was trying to solve up close, and saw the potential right away. She decided to take the risk of helping me, by calling up Yael Benkel for reserve duty at the expense of the total number of reservists she was allotted for any other mission.

Yael Benkel holds a master's degree in National Security Policy Studies from Georgetown University and works as a corporate intelligence researcher in Washington, DC. At the time she served as an intelligence analyst and made great strides as a soldier. She had seen every bit of information that had passed through the base in recent years. A perfect match.

They all agreed to join me for the undertaking after I made it clear that it was not certain something would come out of the project, and we might be reprimanded for wasting time. It was the first time I had hired anyone in my life.

We teamed up and worked off the record, without formal instruction, taking advantage of every spare moment we had.

The other commanders at the base began to realize that something was developing under their noses. A month after getting started, I was surprised to be called to the Base Commander's Forum, which would decide whether I should be allowed to continue with the project, or stop me from any further development. In the entrepreneurial world, this is probably the equivalent of recruiting investors.

The investment was made. They agreed that to allow

me to continue with the project, provided that in one month we would present it to the unit commander.

We had to show results.

The days of grace were over. The presentation was made to the Base Commander, the Unit Commander, and the unit's Chief of Technology. By my side were Noa, Yael and Shlomi. It was probably the longest fifteen minutes of my life up until that moment. At the end of the presentation there was silence.

The unit commander said: "My friends, you have embarked on a groundbreaking project. You have utilized existing resources and created substantial value for the unit. No one around me thought the idea was any good. They claimed it was a waste of time. I am happy to say that they were wrong. I would like now to consider how we can deploy your solution throughout the unit. Thank you very much for your initiative."

Although money was not involved, it was definitely my first startup exit.

CHAPTER 6

Growing Wings

"There's no better time to start than now."

After weeks of self-protective quarantine, I visited my parents. I sat down with my dad for a serious talk about life and development of the venture.

"Dad, listen, I probably managed to find the last piece of the puzzle."

My father replied, "It's wonderful, but you've already set up and are running three other ventures simultaneously. You're working at SOSA, studying for the GMAT so you can get an MBA in the US. You're just one person, how do you think you can do all this successfully?"

He was right, as usual. I've always had a hard time persevering in just one thing. It's all too interesting.

"Dad, this is a very important and intensive project. If it succeeds, it can free us all from quarantine."

"Could be," he answered. "But you need to focus. You can't do everything at once. "

My father, Roni Izaki, has been a real estate entrepreneur for years. Starting out as a young boy picking oranges and avocados in the family orchards and sending them for export, all the way through engineering studies at the Technion and on to establishing projects around the world, he had seen a thing or two, and knew how to grasp reality as it actually is. He is by far the best mentor in the world, and not just because he is my father.

In the next room, my mother was just ending a call: "Thank you Michal, it was nice to talk to you. We'll be in touch soon."

'Hi Mom! I didn't know you were home. Who were you talking to?"

"A very interesting Angel investor, named Michal Tsar-fati-Efrat. I'm going to meet with her next week."

"That's an idea!" my dad jumped in. "Set up a call with Michal. For sure she has the right experience and could guide you through the world of high-tech entrepreneurship and venture capital investments."

That conversation was eye opening.

"Yaniv, you are a serious young man and you sound like you can really contribute with ventures of real value, and not just money. I understand from the goals you outlined to me that you have to choose to be one of the two..."

Choice. I don't like to choose, because it means consciously giving up other opportunities.

"... One choice is to be an entrepreneur in a single venture and pour your soul into it. The second is to be an investor, an Angel. You can invest in several startups with strong entrepreneurs who you believe will be able to achieve the goals, but by definition you will not have a role in those ventures. You will help, make connections, raise funds, but they will run the show. "

Suddenly I realized that the recovered workers and businesses matching venture needs focus to develop, and I was holding it back because I was unable to choose my path.

I called Idan that night, a few hours after the conversation with Michal the Angel investor.

"Idan, do you remember a month ago when I told you that you had found your partner and investor?"

"Of course."

"Look, I believe now is the time to have you take the lead, independently. We have a team of men and women winners who will follow you through fire and water to save the economy, backed by amazing technology that will change the world. I can't give the venture the focus it needs, and I think what preventing progress right now is me. "

"But Yaniv, the reason we started out at all was because I wanted to do a venture together with you. Don't you believe in it anymore?"

"Idan, I do believe in the venture. More than that, I believe in you and the team that will carry it on it. I'm always with you, for advice and guidance, but you have to take hold of the reins. I have to manage my focus differently, or whatever I do will fall to pieces. I've even decided I'll not go for the MBA program anytime soon."

"Are you serious? You've been studying for it like crazy for six months already. Why?"

"Because I found the courage to take action. I thought after the Master's degree I would open a high-tech investment fund, but if I did, that would be at least four years from now. I realized that now was the best time to start, and the graduate degree would only distract me from the goal. There's no better time to start than now. "

"All right, Yaniv, I will accept your decision. It's just important you know that this is our joint project. Even if you give me only advice from now on, it will always be both of us. Maybe I'm the one who called you half-asleep in the middle of the night and told you about a dream I had, but you made it happen."

"Wait, it hasn't even started yet. The essential part of the venture is the execution. An idea, a burning need to be solved and a team are all important, but they are not worth anything without a brilliant execution."

The hard work was still ahead of him. The prime examples of the importance of execution are the social networks, which have always existed, but Facebook's precise implementation of social networking killed MySpace in such a way that it is now studied as a case study in business schools. The users are the ones who will crown the kings of the new world.

"Idan, you can see for yourself what a crazy path we each went through in the last month. We are no longer the same people we were before the pandemic. I have faith that you will succeed, and remember, I am always just a video call away. "

"Thank you, Yaniv, you are a real 'angel.'" Idan winked at me emotionally through a pair of teary eyes. My eyes did not remain dry either.

I had brought the venture to its début. The show now belongs to the entrepreneur.

CHAPTER 7

The Gilded Cage

"Mom, it looks like we'll see each other only in another two weeks or so... I plan to go to the birthday party at the end of the week, but I'll probably have to be in quarantine afterwards."

Thursday night, June 25, 2020. I decided to take a risk and do something I hadn't done in a long time – to leave the house and go to Titi's birthday party. Four months had passed since the Purim celebrations, which had sent me to the first quarantine with a fever and a cough, but with negative test results for the virus.

Titi told me, "I invited only the closest people to me, and I told them there was no way they could come if they had symptoms or were in quarantine... no more than fifty people would come through the door under any circumstances."

That's what you call risk management.

"Hello, who is expecting you?" enquired the masked guard at the entrance to the magnificent apartment building.

"Good evening, I was invited to Titi's birthday, in the penthouse. Has it started yet?"

"People are just now starting to arrive. 47th floor. Enjoy the view."

Kisses. Hugs. Balloons. Flashing lights. Alcohol. Confetti. Smoke. Masks. People.

I had almost forgotten what life looked like.

I woke up the following Tuesday, June 30, 2020, with a barrage of text messages from a friend. There were rumors that, among the people at the party, were several verified virus carriers present, who had no symptoms.

Although I do not tend to believe rumors, this time I made an exception.

"Titi, wake up! You're coming with me. I'll come get you and we'll both go to get tested right away! I'm not waiting... pick you up in half an hour."

"Wait a minute, Izaki, but how do we do that, exactly? You have to have symptoms to get tested."

"Right, that's why we're going to be tested privately. I'm on my way."

When I arrived, Titi was already waiting downstairs, armed with a mask and Alcogel.

"I think we'll skip the hug this time, under the circumstances," she said. I needed no persuading. I opened the car windows and we drove away.

We walked down the empty 2nd floor corridor at Ichilov Hospital. Too many times I had gone through here, but mostly with good results.

"Yes, how can I help you?" asked the receptionist at the entrance to the private lab.

"We came for a field trip!" Titi laughed. The receptionist, not so much.

I cleared my throat and continued: "Well, we are interested in a test for the famous virus."

"Why did you come to be tested? You don't have any symptoms, right? Patients can't show up at the lab just like that!" She said in a threatening tone.

"Obviously we have no symptoms. If we were sick, we wouldn't have left the house... but there was a birthday party and we just..."

"All right, all right, forget it. Do not take off your masks. Fill out these health forms and give me your IDs. Do you want to add a serological blood test for antibodies? It's half price."

A few months ago, I had turned the world upside down to purchase a test for antibodies. Now it was being offered at a discount. Of course, we went for the full package.

"Yaniv, I'm afraid of blood tests," Titi confided to me as we waited to go into the examination room.

"You're joking... If you were scared of needles, how did you get that tattoo on your arm?"

"I did it to overcome the fear. Unfortunately, it didn't work."

A digital announcement blared out: "Patient number A651, come to the nurses' room, thank you." Our turn.

"Come on, it's nothing, I'll go first, and you'll see everything's fine." I must admit that although I had done lots of blood tests, I still wasn't thrilled to do it.

"See? It's easy. Come on, it's your turn," I pointed out the chair for the blood test.

Titi sat down and for a few minutes tried to relax. Every time the nurse approached with the needle, she started gasping for breath and jumping up from the chair in panic.

"I have a phobia of needles! Honestly!" Titi said in a choked-up voice. "Maybe I shouldn't do the test."

"Titi, take a deep breath, close your eyes and in half a minute it will be over." In the end she did it.

The nurse called to us: "Please follow me outside to the garden. We don't do the swab stick tests inside the building."

A stick in the throat. A stick up the nose. A specimen enters an airtight bag labeled "biological hazard."

"You will receive the antibody test results within 48 hours, and a result for the presence of the virus by nightfall."

On the way back home, we wondered if we would get an official message to go into quarantine and if there was a chance that only one of us would be diagnosed with the illness. We also wondered about the reliability of the tests in any case.

18:23. Six hours had passed since the sample was taken, and my phone rang from an unknown number.

"Hello, Yaniv? This is the doctor from the private lab. Your test was found to be positive. You will be contacted by the Ministry of Health and you should now be in quarantine until..."

At this point I could no longer hear any sounds coming from anywhere outside my head.

I replied dryly: "Thanks for the update. I understand. They'll call me. I will stay home. In quarantine. And I have no symptoms. Good night." The call ended. I tried to digest the news.

Immediately after the call ended, Titi sent me a bunch of messages:

"I tested positive"

"Shitttt"

"I'm on the terephone with them"

"Telephone..."

I wrote her that we would be in contact for an update later. We had a lot of people to update that night.

I called my parents: "Hey, Mom? Is Dad there, too? I tested positive."

From that moment on, I was on the phone, messaging and calling, for two whole days. The Ministry of Health, the HMO, family, friends, entrepreneurs.

"Yes, I'm fine, but I think my head and throat are hurting from all the phone calls," I told the HMO nurse.

Quite a few people went into quarantine because of me. The second wave had descended upon them through me.

"No way, Yaniv, I don't believe you! You and Titi actually got infected on her birthday?!" Idan answered in disbelief.

"Yeah, I guess it was meant to be. I got away with it the first round, and apparently pushed my luck."

I chose to take a risk, but you can't win them all. It's part of the game. Need to learn and move on.

"Do you remember telling me at first that this whole thing would go away in three months?" Idan slyly added.

"I remember Idan, I remember it well."

"So, I'm sure you will be glad to know that we have made progress with developing the site... Ah, and Roni also found an important article that explains..."

At that moment I realized that Idan, a man with a dream, had become an entrepreneur.

A few days later I had built myself a quarantine routine. You keep working.

"Hey Dad, is it a good time to show you on a video call new data on some of the startups I've been looking at recently? Unfortunately, half of them are in quarantine because of me, but maybe something good will come out of this experience..."

You are free to go out only after the body has overcome the virus. I chose to act and enjoy every moment in my gilded cage. Quarantine disconnects physical contact, but not the people, and certainly not the entrepreneurial instinct.

EPILOGUE

We are part of a journey that began with the outbreak of a novel plague, which sowed fear and uncertainty in Israel and around the world.

My personal journey began in quarantine. First, when I was exposed at a Purim party to patient 171, and shortly thereafter, when I was sent for further quarantine, this time following exposure to a medical staff member, patient 8344. Finally, in honor of the third quarantine, I was awarded the dubious title of "confirmed patient".

In sum, close to two months in quarantine - all alone, with plenty of time for thoughts that led to a process of internal change.

There is no telling what the fate of the venture will be, but it has already changed the world for me. Uncertainty is the natural state, but the goal is to change the odds in our favor. Live now as if there is no tomorrow, and invest in tomorrow as if we will live forever.

My journey as a tech venture capitalist, also known as "Angel," started in light of the process I have gone through.

You are welcome to join. Together, we will meet the challenges of the changing reality.

Yaniv Izaki, Angel. Investing in people.

GRATITUDE

Thanks to the heroes of my story. Each and every one of you has changed my life in one way or another, whether through years of friendship or merely in a single conversation.

A big thank you to my family for their support and love during this challenging time.

To my brother Amir, who constantly reveals to me the power of perseverance of purpose; to my sister Carmel, who teaches me to see the world in a new way through our conversations, and to laugh at life.

To my mother Yael, through whom I learned to see women as a strategic advantage and to my father Roni, my mentor and advisor who always wants me to be my best.

Yaniv